B.C.—Big Wheel

Johnny Hart

CORONET BOOKS
Hodder Fawcett Ltd., London

Copyright © 1963, 1964 by
Publishers News Syndicate, Inc.
Copyright © 1969 by
Fawcett Publications, Inc. New York
First published 1969 by
Fawcett Publications Inc.
New York
Coronet edition 1973

Printed and bound in Great Britain for
Coronet Books,
Hodder Fawcett Ltd,
St. Paul's House, Warwick Lane,
London, EC4P 4AH
by Hazell Watson & Viney Ltd,
Aylesbury, Bucks

ISBN 0 340 16880 3

OL' JOHN WILL BE GLAD TO SEE ME. HE NEVER KNOWS WHAT TO DO WITH HIMSELF WHEN I'M AWAY ON VACATION.

I'M ALMOST THERE. ...STRANGE, ...I DON'T REMEMBER THAT VOLCANO. ....AND DIDN'T THAT CREEK USED TO RUN EAST AND WEST?

..NOT A CAVE IN SIGHT ANYWHERE, ..MUST HAVE FILLED THEM IN.
IT NEVER FAILS,-

YOU GO AWAY FOR TWO WEEKS AND THEY CHANGE EVERYTHING AROUND.

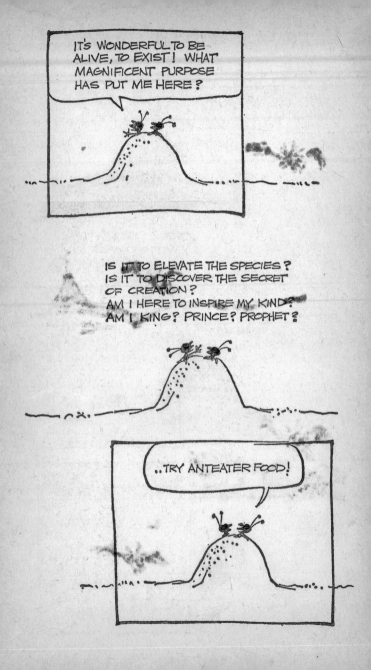

DEAR SNAKE PLEASE DO US
THE HONOR OF APPEARING AT
OUR OPENING GAME TO THROW
OUT THE FIRST BALL.

WHENEVER PEOPLE TAKE ADVANTAGE OF ME, I WANT TO SMASH THINGS!
THERE,.. SEE! NOW THAT YOU'VE TALKED ABOUT IT, THE URGE IS GONE. YOU'RE CURED!
DR. PETER HEAD SHRINKER
IT'S A COMFORT TO RETIRE AT NIGHT KNOWING THAT YOU HAVE HELPED SOMEONE TO....?
WHAM
CRUNCH
ZAK
GNISH
DR.

HAVE YOU EVER SEEN ANYONE STARVE? -- FIRST THE PAINS, THEN THE BLOATING OF THE STOMACH, THEN THE SWELLING OF THE TONGUE, ... IT'S AWFUL!
REPULSIVE TONGUE OR NO REPULSIVE TONGUE, -THIS POOR FELLOW NEEDS TO EAT!
EEEUUGGHH
ZOT

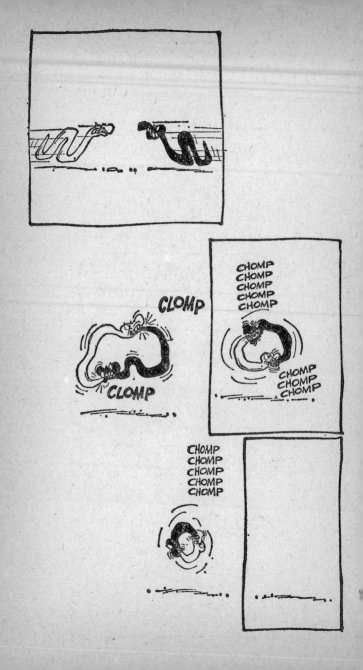

THE WORM!

'FEET WENT TO SLEEP.

ZIP

BLAAAT

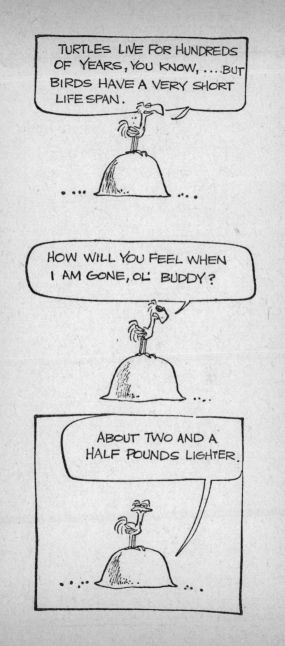

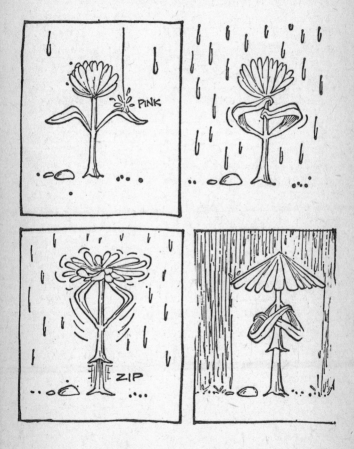